Man at Arms

Poems from the First World War

James Arthur Morton

All rights reserved

No part of this publication may be reproduced, stored in a retrieval system, or transmitted in any form by any means, electronic, mechanical, photocopying, recording or otherwise, without the prior permission of The Handsel Press Ltd

British Library Cataloguing in Publication Data:
a catalogue record for this publication
is available from the British Library

ISBN   978-1-917841-01-6

© A.E. Morton 2025

The right of A.E. Morton to be identified as the editor of this work has been asserted by her in accordance with the Copyright, Designs and Patents Act 1988

Typeset in 11pt Minion Pro at Haddington, Scotland

Cover and Printing by West Port Print, St Andrews

CONTENTS

Exordium 1916	5
Invocation	6
Supplication	7
To All the Unborn Dead	8
The Word	9
Fatherhood	9
The Soldier	10
Asleep	11
Christmas 1916	12
Francis Ledwidge	13
The World's Tragedy	14
The Romantic School	15
The Traveller	16
Spring 1918	17
Sunrise	18
The Garden	18
Evening	19
Night	19
Tragedy	20

In memory of a talented grandfather

James Arthur Morton, known as Arthur, was born in 1878 in Manchester, where he grew up and served his apprenticeship as an electrical engineer at W.T. Glover & Co. He later went to work for British Insulated Cables at Prescot and married Annie Elizabeth Lindley in 1903. They were both Swedenborgians, members of the New Church, but later joined the Church of England. They moved from Prescot to Huyton and their two children were brought up there. Their son Alan became a botanist and mycologist, their daughter Dorothy became a vet.

Some of Arthur's poetry was published in *The Link* and he wrote humorous poems and articles about electrical engineering which featured in Glover's inhouse magazine and *The Electrical Engineer*. He was also a talented artist, using pencil and water colours to draw local views around Prescot and at their various holiday venues. He died in 1938 so neither his daughter-in-law nor his grandchildren ever knew him. His widow lived until 1969, a much-loved mother and grandmother. He lived on in oral memory, his poetry and artwork.

According to family tradition, he was responsible for the pencil drawing of his own father-in-law, William Lindley, which is on the front cover – it is called 'A Man at Arms'.

Exordium —1916

What though 'tis Wintertide with us, and winds
Of disappointment beat against our faith;
Though friends, departed, speak to us no more,
And glowing fires but light our lonely hearths –
We are not less the chidren of this land,
Nor can aught kill the spirit of our race,
Or tear from out life's book our history,
Staunch will we stand, due service give, for those
Who mourn their shattered homes and desolate fields
Laid waste; and for the sake of this dear land
Our heritage fair, set in th' encircling sea;
Steadfast for freedom, knowing naught of fear;
Undaunted.   For though Death's imperious voice
Call thousands onward ere the task is done,
We shall awaken from this dream of strife
Into the promise of a newborn day.

Published in *The Link*, December 31st, 1915

Invocation

Pluck out thy hate, O Heart,
Renew they life;
Fling forth thy bitterness,
Reck not the strife,
Trample thine anger out,
Be merciful;
Just is the perfect Heart
And pitiful.
Dare to be generous,
Wait and forgive;
For all the Dead have died
That thou might live.
O Heart, be patient yet;
War shall be ended,
And love with shining eyes
Out of the darkness rise
Deathless and splendid.

Supplication

Keep Thou my feet –
If I should stray into the wild.
Be gentle with thy erring child,
And guide me.

If in the strife
I fight not with the single heart,
Or take, alas, th'ignoble part,
Forsake me not.

If anger, Lord,
Impels my passionate hand to strike,
If in sheer might I take delight,
Restrain me, Lord.

And when at last,
The daylight's gone,
And all alone
I pass into that Valley cold,
Groping for some dear hand to hold,
Take Thou my hand
Within thine own –
Lord hold me fast.

(An Imitation of one of Wm Canton's poems)

To All the Unknown Dead

Mute are your fervent lips
    that once with laughter rang;
Fast closed the shining eyes
    from whence your light was shed;
Hushed now those cheerful songs
    which, eloquent, you sang;
And cold your passionate hearts
    whose earthly love lies dead.

Folded the dauntless hands
    that clasped the guns and swords;
Finished the ecstacy
    of striving in the fight;
To dust resolved, the tongues
    which once spoke flowing words,
And all your rosy hopes
    drowned in relentless night –
You are at peace, asleep
    beneath the earth and sky,
Unknown, unsung, amid
    this battle of the strong.

But no! you entered into Life, you did not die,
Your Valour lives for ever in triumphant Song.

Written December 1915, the year of the great war

The Word

Going away to fight,
He wrung my hand and said
"Good-bye,
I shall not die" . . .
I prayed his word was right.

All falteringly, I said
"Adieu! . . ."
My word's come true:
God keeps him – he is dead.

Fatherhood

The wind is whispering in the trees
The leaves talk quietly;
I wish that you were here, dear lad,
Speaking to me.

Come with the winds across the sea,
Over its silver foam;
Give me your hand, O Son of mine;
Come home, come home!

* * * *

Alas! his feet are turned aside,
To me he will not come;
I shall not hear his voice again –
He has gone Home.

Published in the *Manchester City News*, Sept. 30th, 1916

The Soldier

"Though He slay me, yet will I trust in Him" (Job 13: 15)

O Father mine – the sounding bugle blows,
And calls me forth to fight . . .
I do not joyfully take up the sword;
Yet I would strike for Liberty and Life,
Though not for mine alone.
My life is not my own – no freehold given
To use for my short-sighted ends;
But a great leasehold loaned by Thee,
In trust, to keep it clean and use it right,
This is the task Thou gavest me –
I do not want to lay it down.
Yet it is hard to live for Thee,
Is it so hard to die? . . .
My life is Thine; and if Thou so decree,
I will resign it back to Thee,
Trustfully, willingly.

Published in *The Christian Commonwealth*, November 1916

Asleep

I used to call her out to watch with me
The sunset flaming forth across the lea,
Or filmy mists come stealing o'er the ground –
To hear the thrush its vesper song rehearse,
Or the bold blackbird fling its sonorous verse
Upon the evening air, through which the sound
Found a glad way right to the listener's heart.

All this is done with: I shall call no more.
I cannot call her through the earthbound door
That shuts her in. She lies asleep, in bed
Of dusty mould, and grass grows o'er her head:
She takes her rest, but there is none for me.
She will not come, and I ask bitterly
When I may go.   Hers is the better part.

Written November 1916

Christmas 1916

"That ye might have Life and have it more abundantly."
(John 10: 10)

Now that dark Winter broods upon the land,
And many, sorrowing, fear to face
This Christmastide that lacks the gift of Peace;
We needs must stand a little while
And think of all the host of fearless men
Who have for England died . . . For us they bled:
Kinsmen of ours, stronghearted to the end;
We are their brothers in our love of them.

So, for their sake, and with a firmer faith,
Let courage turn our heavy grief's lament
Into thanksgiving for those valiant Dead,
Who died that we might still for England live.

For *The Link*

Francis Ledwidge

(Killed in France, July 31, 1917)

Where dream you now, O gentle youthful heart?
Your second youth has come; where do you dwell?
See you once more the loved green hills of Eire
Standing beside those streams you sung so well?

Ah me! you've found the garden – Tirnanogue;
Where trees and flowers blossomed in God's mind
Before they grew in fields or poets' verse:
Where your own black-bird first called down the wind.

Written August 6th, 1917

Published in *The Herald* September 1st, 1917

The World's Tragedy

"Dead bodies were heaped there, buried and unburied. Men dug into corruption when they tried to dig a trench. Men sat on dead bodies when they peered through their periscopes. They ate and slept with the stench of death in their nostrils. Below them were the enemy's mine shafts . . . and men fought like devils with bombs and and bayonets over mine craters which had buried another score or so of them. The story of Hooge was a serial carried on from week to week, but the place was only one of our little schools of war for bright young men."
(From *Battles of the Somme* by Philip Gibbs)

What bloodshot fabric this, woven of human suffering:
The dreadful pattern stares, limned in uttermost horror,
A dark and livid shroud of agony and death . . .
And yet revealing too, all the deathless valour,
The soul's deep discipline, the supreme endurance,
Of those who fought this fight.

Surely their sacrifice, stedfast courage, patience,
Are attributes divine . . . But O great God of right,
What ghastly tragedy this, that the full use of these
Great qualities sublime, should maim and crucify
The men they glorify.

Written February 1917

Published in *The Herald*, April 7th, 1917

Poem opposite: written August 1917
Published in *The Herald*, September 1st, 1917

The Romantic School

Green meadows, torn and seared to dirty brown:
Farmhouses once with patient labour built
To shelter busy peaceful men,
Now mere amorphous heaps of stone:
The whispering sun-barred coppices
Dumb crowds of jagged splintered stumps:
A wasted, tortured land of death . . .

What of the fighting-men, living in muck
And wet, and filthy clothes . . . ?
Nagging uncertainty, black fear for them,
And sudden gripings at the heart:
Faces of pain, windowing hunted souls:
Unutterable weariness:
Thin mirthless laughter, pitiful,
Rasping from twisted lips:
Teeth set on edge by droning shells
That rake the shivering air:
And peering eyes shot from the day
Into a starless night:
Shattered, tormented and distorted limbs:
Men buried quick, under a headlong spate
Of shell-thrown earth, life stifled out:
Brains spattered in the trench:
And bloody corpses sprawling in the waste.
And every corpse a husband or a son.

These things, O God, we call
The Glamour and Romance of War.

The Traveller

So I set out, nor bade Him a farewell
On that so-long-anticipated day,
Nor recked I aught of heaven nor yet of hell;
Sufficient that I took the long highway ...

And when I ran with unreluctant feet,
Consuming swift the pleasures of the way,
Racing fast through the hours so bitter-sweet;
He call me back to Him: I said Him nay.

Or when I loitered in disdainful ease
On flowered banks that lipped the roadway's brim,
He walked in front beckoning me on to Him:
I did not go . . . .
                But near the journey's end,
When deep within the Vale, shadowy and dim,
I went afraid, yet all too proud to call,
Groping amid that darkness none may rend;
He took my hand so that I might not fall.
And gently, firmly, drew me home with Him.

Written April 4th, 1917

Spring 1918

A day of English Spring,
When thrushes sing!
The air is soft and warm
As Love's white arm.
A high, faint breeze,
Moving above the highest trees,
Shepherds with gentle hands, a few
White clouds across the blue.
Celandine too,
Scatters its yellow stars
Between the elms, among the bars
Of sunlight. Flush
With roadway's lip blush
Shy campions by the hedge:
Even the sedge
Is glad to greet the Sun . . .
And I am glad
That spring has come:
Then sad,
That Spring will soon be gone.
And then –
I think of all the men
Who'll never come home again;
Who'll never feel an English Spring again.

Written March 23rd, 1918

Sunrise

Symbol of Love and Might,
Through the burning gates of Dawn
The Golden Day strides in . . .
Down the uplands, through the corn,
Over the jewelled fields,
With fiery-sandalled shimmering feet
And glowing eyes, he yields
To none . . . With flaming rays unfurled
He steeps the sleeping world
In glorious wonderworking Light.

The Garden

"Now in the place where he was crucified there was a garden." (John 19: 41)

Where men are dying
In agony of doubt and fear
On the torn earth's bosom lying,
There's still a garden near;
In which the Master waits,
Beckoning the crucified
To enter thro' His widely-opened gates,
And touch His hands and side.

Written June 6th, 1918

Evening

Down sinks the sun,
The hills to purple turn:
The corn to gold,
Reddened by bars of light
Which steal between the trees
To sunward.
A cloud of smoke,
Light blue 'gainst darker green,
Rises before the wood
Upon the night.
The fragrant air is still:
Only a solitary bird
Calls faintly from behind:
Then all is quiet,
And earth is steeped in peace.

Written August 13th, 1918

Night

I am so tired . . .
I drag my heavy feet
Along the way.
Dim is my sight,
I cannot see the light
Of coming day . . .
Lend me Thine eyes,
O let me have Thy call;
Then, though my foot should slip,
I cannot fall.

Written October 1918

Tragedy

Youth was my Golden Age:
When life was full and fine,
Open and free . . .

The ways stood clean and clear,
In those full-blooded hours . . .

I know it now,
But then I knew it not:
I was too near to clearly see . . .

'Tis only now I feel the certain thrill
When I remember –
When my Youth is gone . . .
Yes! now my practised soul
Has grown full sensitive;
My future moulded so
That I could finely penetrate
Youth's very core, taste it,
Know what it really was:
Now I grow old . . .

Written August 20th, 1918